Hellifield

& its Railways

Hellifield

& its Railways

Andrew Wilson

TEMPUS

First published 2001
Copyright © Andrew R. Wilson, 2001

Tempus Publishing Limited
The Mill, Brimscombe Port,
Stroud, Gloucestershire, GL5 2QG
www.tempus-publishing.com

ISBN 0 7524 2357 6

Typesetting and origination by
Tempus Publishing Limited
Printed in Great Britain by
Midway Colour Print, Wiltshire

Dedication

To my wife, Chris
For all the happy years we spent living in Hellifield
And to the late Donald Palmer
Who inspired this book

Contents

Introduction

There are few places in the old West Riding part of Yorkshire where the Pennines can be crossed at lower than 1,000 ft. One of these is the Aire Gap, which traverses the 610 ft watershed between the rivers Aire and Ribble. With Skipton at the eastern end and Hellifield to the west, both settlements date back to Saxon times and the Danelaw. The name Hellifield itself derives from the Old English, *Helga-Feld* meaning Halga's Field or possibly the Holy Field. By 1086 the Domesday Book records the settlement as Helegfeld, and by 1203 the name had become Helwefeld.

Hellifield changed very little until the 1830s. The hamlet with a population of around 250 people was an agricultural community that augmented its income with cottage weaving, initially wool but later cotton. In 1831 there were a mere thirty-five cottages clustered around the Keighley & Kendal Turnpike Road, where the most exciting event was the changing of the mail coach's horses at the Black Horse Inn.

In 1844 surveyors working for the North Western Railway appeared in Hellifield. They were surveying a route to link the Leeds & Bradford Railway at Skipton to the Lancaster & Carlisle Railway, later to become part of the London & North Western Railway, at Low Gill. Parliamentary approval for this line was granted on 26 June 1846, but it was to be February 1848 before the navvies descended on Hellifield. Despite appalling weather during the winter of 1848-49, the 'Little' North Western Railway was able to open its Skipton to Ingleton line on 30 July 1849.

The station provided at Hellifield was situated 400 yards north east of the village, where the railway crossed Haw Lane. A small single-storey building was provided, constructed of wood and plaster with mock Tudor styling. It was dwarfed by a substantial detached house provided for the station master. The first holder of this position was William Ash who was paid £44 4s 0d a year, and expected to work a minimum of thirteen hours a day, seven days a week. A small goods yard was provided with cattle pens and coal staithes.

For thirty years, the railway had little significant effect on the population of Hellifield, with the census returns showing only a dozen men employed on average. However, the aspirations of both the Midland Railway and Lancashire & Yorkshire Railway were about to change this once and for all. Determined to secure its own route to Scotland, free from the petty restrictions imposed by the L.N.W.R., the Midland embarked upon its ambitious Settle & Carlisle scheme. After Parliament refused permission to abandon the line in April 1869, the scene was set for momentous changes at Hellifield. 1871 saw the Midland purchase the North Western Railway while the Lancashire & Yorkshire Railway was actively engaged in completing work on its Chatburn to Hellifield extension.

With the imminent arrival of the Lancashire & Yorkshire at Hellifield, thoughts turned to what format the junction should take. A triangular layout was favoured but costs mitigated against it, and eventually a trailing junction was decided upon, which was completed by May 1879. However, the opening of the new junction was delayed because the contract to build the new joint station was not permitted until February 1879.

The new station was built a quarter of a mile to the west of the North Western building. It was provided with a carriage shed, exchange sidings and an engine shed. The Lancashire & Yorkshire built an engine shed of its own together with extensive sidings in the triangle of land created by the junction. Both companies provided terraced housing for their employees.

Midland Terrace comprised forty three-bedroom dwellings while Lancashire & Yorkshire provided just eight. Neither terrace was built of local stone, the railway companies preferring to BRing in cheaper materials. For its stationmaster and shed foreman, the Midland built a pair of substantial semi-detached houses, Station Villas, opposite the subway entrance to the station. Gas lighting was also provided along Midland Terrace, the gas being provided by the company's own gasworks.

By 1895 Hellifield's population had increased considerably. Of the 104 houses in the village, sixty-five were occupied by railway families. Many of the remaining homes took in lodgers who worked on the railway. However, housing was still at a premium and was to remain so until the developments at Thorndale Street, Brook Street, Old Station Road (Haw Lane) and Kendal Road were completed in the early 1900s. After being appointed as a ticket collector, Jack Holmes was forced to cycle to and from Colne every day for six months before being given a house in Lancashire & Yorkshire Terrace. Of the householders at this time, 32% were engine drivers and only 2% were firemen. The inhabitants of the village were now a cosmopolitan mix with representatives from over half of England's counties as well as a fair mix of Welsh, Irish and Scots. A certain James Payne hailed from the West Indies. Between 1871 and 1881 the village's population increased by 88%, while over the next two decades it rose by 42% and 30% respectively.

At the turn of the century the station was handling some 36,000 passengers a year. Livestock and mineral traffic was substantial and generating a healthy income, thereby recouping handsomely the Midland Railway's initial investments of £11,000 on the station complex, £7,000 on the engine shed and £2,718 on houses. Not surprisingly the Midland was the largest single rate-payer in the village with a gross valuation of £2,495, which gave a rateable value of £1,872 a year.

The spiritual well-being of the village was catered for by an Anglican church, St Aidan's, consecrated in 1906; a Baptist chapel; an Evangelical chapel; a Railway Mission, which looked after the welfare of young men in lodgings; and a Temperance Mission. The WHSmith book-stall on the station sorted and delivered newspapers throughout the village. The Hellifield Co-operative Society was paying a healthy dividend of two shillings in the pound.

Before 1906 primary school children shared the same premises as the Anglican Church in, what is now, The Institute. As the population grew, the church school became more and more overcrowded. Eventually plans were drawn up for a new school and, on 1 April 1915, the old school closed with the new one opening to pupils on 7 April.

Traffic and revenue continued to rise until the outbreak of war in August 1914. The post war period Brought eventual rationalisation and a slow decline as the L.M.S. closed the Lancashire & Yorkshire engine shed. Yet in the 1930s Hellifield boasted three grocers, a post office, two butchers, two confectioners, a cobbler, two barbers, a blacksmith, two garages and a tailor, Mr Aherne.

Hellifield remained a railway village until the 1960s. At the end of L.M.S. ownership a repair shop was built, but the gradual run down of the railway broke irrevocably the once close link between railway and village. The engine shed was closed on 17 June 1963 and demolished in 1972 after being used to store locomotives destined for preservation. The station was reduced to the status of an unmanned halt as an air of desolation and neglect descended on the once busy complex. Most of the younger railwaymen left the railway or moved away to find work. In the 1980s demolition of the station was narrowly avoided after preservation as a Grade II listed building. The station and canopy were eventually renovated and are potent reminders of the once rich railway heritage of the village.

The author wishes to acknowledge the valuable assistance of R.M. Casserley in allowing access to his father's photographs of Hellifield, and to the late Jim Davenport for providing so many of the images used in this book. He also wishes to thank Mr John Lassey, headmaster of Hellifield Primary School, for allowing him access to the school records and Mike Steele, his predecessor, for collecting so much information about the village.

One
The Village of Hellifield

Architecturally, the village of Hellifield is a fascinating mixture of styles: agricultural, railway and post railway. The seventeenth and eighteenth century buildings were swamped by Victorian and Edwardian developments, resulting from the industrialization of the rural community. Railway developments in the 1880s increased the population, bringing new housing, a parish church and a larger primary school. Council houses followed in the 1920s and the 1930s brought semi-detached houses to Kendal Road and The Green.

A wintry scene in Midland Terrace during the days of Midland Railway. The tree-lined road leads to the 1880 junction station. Ever conscious of its responsibilities to its employees, the Midland provided them with well-built, quality homes.

Hellifield County Primary School under construction in late 1914. The new school was needed to accommodate the growing number of children in the village. Built on the Settle side of the village, it opened its doors to pupils at 9a.m. on 7 April 1915.

The Settle Road in 1912 with the semi-detached houses Rockville and Glendair under construction. On the left at the end of Midland Terrace are the four houses known as Pendle View, with John Hoar's grocer's shop just visible. Settle Road is now known as Kendal Road.

To house its employees, the Midland Railway built forty substantial 3-bedroom homes at a cost of £2,718. Each had a small front garden and a slightly larger back yard. The wooden fencing and trees illustrate the lengths to which the railway company was prepared to go in order to look after its work force. Gas lighting was provided, the first in the village, because of the shift work demanded by the railway.

A summer's day in Midland Terrace during L.M.S. days. Apart from the L.M.S. signpost and fewer trees, little has changed from the 1900s. Considerable use was made of concrete blocks in constructing the houses, and the exposed rear windows were double-glazed. Number 13 was used as a library and reading room, in conjunction with the engine shed's mutual improvement classes.

Station Villas, opposite the subway entrance to the junction station, was not completed until after Midland Terrace. Provided for the station master and shed foreman, the first occupants were Robert Tudor and G. Jackson.

Brook Street is pictured shortly after completion c.1910. This row of privately built terraced houses is on the opposite side of the Settle Road from Midland Terrace, which can be seen in the distance.

Water Bridge, where the Settle Road crosses Hellifield Beck, in early 1914 with the Duke of Wellington's Regiment recruitment march in full swing. In the background to the right is the Lancashire & Yorkshire Railway's engine-shed. The field behind the marching soldiers is the site of the wooden shacks put up to house the navvies who built the railway, the last of which was demolished in 1910.

Water Bridge in the foreground, and Town End Bridge looking east towards Main Street, c. 1910. On the embankment is the Lancashire & Yorkshire Railway's signal-box that controlled entry into the company's engine shed and exchange sidings.

Like the Midland Railway, the Lancashire & Yorkshire Railway had to provided housing for its workers. Lancashire & Yorkshire Terrace was a more modest affair than Midland Terrace comprising only eight houses. The lane leads to the company's engine shed.

Main Street in the 1920s, looking west towards Town End Bridge which carries the Lancashire & Yorkshire's mainline to Chatburn and Blackburn. The Temperance Hotel, opened in 1890, is on the right along with Craven Terrace and the Post Office.

The junction of Main Street and the Gisburn Road. Behind the houses on the right is Hellifield Auction Mart, which was to generate considerable cattle traffic for both the Midland and Lancashire & Yorkshire railways. Just visible on the left is the Black Horse Hotel.

The Black Horse Hotel stands at the corner of Gisburn Road and Main Street. When the mail-coaches ran along the Keighley to Settle Turnpike Road, the horses were changed here. The entry to the stable yard is just to the left.

From further down Gisburn Road, the whole frontage of the Black Horse is clearly seen. On the right is Rose Cottage, one of the eighteenth century weavers' cottages.

Rose Cottage is one of Hellfield's oldest surviving buildings. It is typical of weavers' cottages found throughout the West Riding part of Yorkshire. Behind was a weaving shed which was demolished in the nineteenth century.

Hellifield's Railway Mission was a little further down Gisburn Road. It is representative of its genre with mock Tudor walls and a corrugated roof. The Mission had been established to look after the welfare of young men who came to the village in search of railway work.

The Baptist Sunday School was also built on Gisburn Road. At one time Hellifield could boast no less than four places of worship. The only denomination not represented was the Roman Catholic Church.

The Grange was also known as The Vicarage while it was the home of the curate-in-charge of Hellifield. Before the construction of St Aidan's, Anglican services were held in the school-room on Main Street. After being empty for a while, it became the home of a Mr Grundy who changed its name to The Grange.

Hellifield Peel in the 1920s was the ancestral home of the Hammerton family, the lords of the Manor of Hellifield. In 1440 Henry VI granted Laurence Hammerton a licence to fortify and embattle Hellifield Peel. The last male Hammerton, Chisnall, died in 1908 and is buried in Long Preston Church. The Peel then became the home of William Nicholson, a former Lord Mayor of Leeds.

After the death of William Nicholson during the Second World War, the Peel was requisitioned to house prisoners of war. Once these had been repatriated, no buyer could be found and so Tot Lord stripped the interior taking it to Settle. Consequently, the house fell into disrepair and is now a shell, the wings having been demolished. There are tentative plans to restore the building to its 1930s condition.

St Aidan's Church was consecrated in 1906; the cost of £3,500 having been raised by public subscription. Built by John Carr & Sons of Long Preston to the plans of Messrs Connon & Chorley of Leeds, each stone was hand cut on site.

Opposite St Aidan's is the new vicarage which replaced The Grange, located on the corner of Haw Lane (Old Station Road) and Skipton Road. Auction Mart Farm is just visible behind the tree.

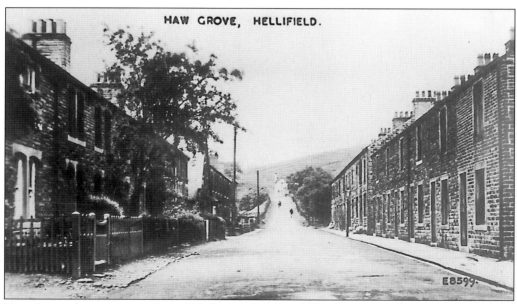

Haw Grove, known variously as Old Station Road and Haw Lane, was the access road to the 'Little' North Western Railway station and Hellifield Haw, a round-topped hill overlooking the village. The station master's house is in the middle distance.

Thorndale Road was built off Skipton Road during the second decade of the twentieth century. The 1849 station and house are in the middle distance.

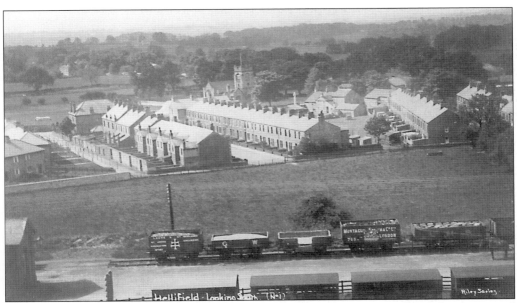

Haw Lane and Thorndale Street with St Aidan's Church c.1920. The foreground is dominated by the 'Little' North Western's goods yard, which remained open until the late 1920s when the cattle docks were moved onto the site of the Lancashire & Yorkshire Railway's engine shed.

THE SWINGS. HELLIFIELD.

Council houses first appeared in Hellifield in the 1920s. Built on the Skipton side of the village, they were carefully laid out around a green on which children's swings were provided.

As motorists entered the village they would be confronted by this view descending Hellifield Hill. On the right are the council houses while the first building on the left would be St Aidan's Church.

Two

Midland and Lancashire
& Yorkshire Days

The opening of the junction between the Lancashire & Yorkshire Railway's Chatburn line and the Midland Railway's Leeds to Settle Junction route changed irrevocably the face of Hellifield. What had once been a rural backwater over night became an important railway junction with a large station, two engine sheds, three signal-boxes and extensive sidings. Between 1851 and 1895 the population increased from 273 to 672, as rows of terrace houses were built to accommodate the influx of railwaymen and their families.

The 'Little' North Western Railway's Hellifield station was at the top of Haw Lane (Old Station Road). The wooden building was dwarfed by the station master's house, whose first occupant was William Ash. He was paid seventeen shillings a week to act as station master, booking clerk, porter, signalman, shunter and agent. Standing by the signal in this 1890s view is gate keeper, Mr Charles Salt.

Approaching Hellifield in the up direction this was a driver's view shortly after the junction station was opened in 1880. The Midland's four road engine shed is to the left with the sand house chimney prominent. Between the signal gantry is the wooden coal stage and to the right is North Junction signalbox.

The junction with the Lancashire & Yorkshire was on the Skipton side of the station. In this 1906 view, the first South Junction signal box is seen by the down running lines. The Blackburn line bay is occupied by empty stock. The Trubshaw-designed buildings are masked by the extensive canopies. The layout of the well-kept track was designed by the District PM Inspector Mr Carter.

The elegant glazed awnings extended over 100ft beyond the buildings. The metal columns and brackets were cast by MacFarlanes of Glasgow, and featured the Midland's MR monogram and Wyvern heraldic device.

The Midland engine shed was also designed at Derby by Trubshaw. It was a standard four road dead-end shed. Built to the north of the up mainline, the buildings and yard cost £7,000 to construct. In this late 1890s view, Johnson 1808 class 4-4-0 No.82 awaits its next working.

Several platform staff wait for an up arrival at 1.58p.m. The engine shed and coal stack are in the background. The small wooden building on the left was used by the ticket collectors. Both the MR monogram and Wyvern are visible in the ironwork.

WHSmith had a book-stall on the up platform outside the ladies' first class waiting-room. Newspapers, periodicals, books and postcards were sold and boys with trays of merchandise were employed to sell them to passengers as trains arrived.

The Midland was proud of its achievements, and staff photographs were very much part of the company's ethos. Here Hellifield's platform staff are posing along with the book-stall staff, around the turn of the century.

The down platform, No.2, looks remarkably quiet. The station was built by Robert Leake of Normanton. The LYR was granted running powers and was charged rent for the use of the station. Passenger trains were not allowed in the loops, only empty stock and goods.

The LYR's engine shed was spacious with a well-thought out layout. The three-road shed was typical of Barton-Wright's thinking, and was provided with a coal-hole and turntable. In this view taken between 1905 and 1912, an Aspinall Radial 2-4-2T is by the coal-hole.

LYR 0-6-0 No. 383 is along side the shed's sand house, c. 1914-18. Joe Sayer is on the running plate, Teddy Earnshaw is on the cab steps, while Fred and Jack Shorrock are in the cab. The embankment behind carries the Midland mainline.

Both sheds' staff maintained all types of rolling stock, including wagons with their primitive fat axle boxes. In the LYR high level sidings, Teddy Waterhouse, 'Fatty Lad' Arthur and David Greenwood are attending to a Midland 5-plank wagon, which has suffered a hot box.

An immaculate LYR 0-6-0 No.57 (L.M.S. No. 12260, B.R. No. 52260) is on the LYR shed's 50ft turntable. Built in 1894 No.57 was not withdrawn until April 1961. The site of the LYR shed is now a housing estate.

Johnson 1327 4-4-0 No.311 is stabled outside the Midland's wooden carriage shed during the Great War. Women cleaners were employed while the men were away fighting. Behind No.311 is a grounded Midland Pullman car, which was used as a mess for the cleaners.

A close-up of the Pullman with another set of war-time cleaners. On the left is the aptly named Maggie Persil. As soon as the men returned from active duty, the women found themselves out of work.

The Midland shed was allocated a steam breakdown crane. It is seen at work with the Skipton crane dealing with a derailment at Long Preston in 1916, in front of an appreciative audience.

Despite having their own shed, LYR locomotives sometimes went onto the Midland depot. A fully-coaled LYR 4-4-0 No.985 is waiting on one of the shed roads opposite the station to take over an up working over the Blackburn line.

Johnson 1808 Class 4-4-0 is being turned on the Midland shed's 50ft Cowans & Sheldon turntable. The elegance of the Johnson design is only too apparent in this view.

Few views survive of locomotives shunting the ex-NWR's goods yard. This one is of Johnson 0-6-0 No.2116, seen with its driver, fireman, shunter and guard.

Three

The L.M.S.
1923-1947

After the Grouping in 1923, the L.M.S. found itself with two medium-sized engine sheds at Hellifield. To nobody's great surprise, the smaller LYR shed was closed in 1927, and the cattle docks serving the Auction Mart were moved there from the North Western station. In 1935 Hellifield became a garage shed under Leeds Holbeck. The gas lighting was replaced by electricity, a water softening plant installed and, in 1940, a new 60 foot turntable was provided and the Midland shed roof was replaced. December 1945 saw plans drawn up to modernize the shed, but nationalization put them on hold. The period also saw a gradual transition from Midland practices to those of William Stanier.

Severe winter weather in the high Pennines usually meant one thing, snow. The Settle & Carlisle was particularly susceptible to drifting at Stainforth and Dent. Consequently, Hellifield was well provided with snowploughs. Here, in the mid-1930s, an intermediate plough is seen attached to a Midland 0-6-0, to the right can be seen one of the large Midland bogie ploughs which were withdrawn around this time.

W.A. Camwell photographed the L.Y.R. shed in 1930, three years after its closure. The new cattle dock for the Auction Mart traffic is to the left. The shed itself is typical of Barton-Wright's practice with its hipped roof and prominent foreman's office.

One of the Midland's bogie snowploughs is stabled at the rear of the Midland shed in early L.M.S. days. When first built, these impressive pieces of rolling stock were painted in crimson lake livery. Despite their size, the ploughs were not very effective, being prone to derailment.

2P 4-4-0 No.456 is in immaculate lined L.M.S black livery. Captured on film by Henry Casserley on 30 June 1933, the locomotive is typical of the secondary passenger classes allocated to Hellifield at this time.

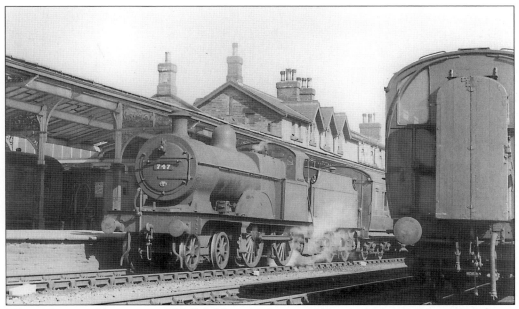

When Norman Glover visited Hellifield on 14 August 1939, motive power was still predominantly pre-Grouping, as the following six views illustrate. Here, re-built Johnson 3P 4-4-0 No.747 is in charge of a down local. Passenger stock has been stabled in the down cripple siding. The station canopies are still in their 1880 condition.

Deeley re-built many of the Johnson designs, such as 3F 0-6-0 No. 3192. Stabled on the turntable road, which also doubled as a preparation siding, No.3192 awaits its next turn. These Belpaire boilered 0-6-0s were synonymous with Hellifield's freight and trip duties for the best part of seventy-five years.

Johnson's 6ft 9in 3P 4-4-0s were also an integral part of the Hellifield scene for almost fifty years. No.734 is on the coal road and will have just had its fire cleaned before replenishing its tender from the coal stage.

Ex-L.Y.R. locomotives regularly worked into Hellifield from the Blackburn line and were turned and serviced on the Midland shed. Aspinall 3F 0-6-0 No. 12157 (B.R. No.52157) has been coaled and the fireman is on the tender about to top the tank up with water.

3F 0-6-0 No.3235 has been left on the sand house siding while the crew mash their tea in the mess. The feather of steam at the safety valve suggests that the locomotive will soon move off shed to take up its next working.

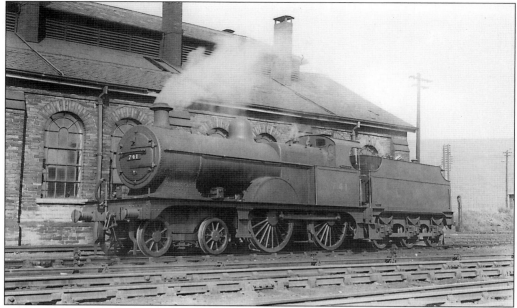

4-4-0 No.741 occupies the same position as No.3235. The Midland shed, by now almost sixty years old, looks in remarkably good condition with the pointing, roof and windows all being well maintained.

As with most steam sheds, Hellifield was used to house stored locomotives until they could be called into works for either an overhaul or scrapping. 3P 4-4-0 No.773 has the tell-tale sack over the chimney and the tender has been emptied of coal.

A small number of Stanier 3P 2-6-2Ts were allocated to Hellifield. No.183 is passing the site of the 'Little' North Western station *c.*1945 with a local stopping train to either Ingleton or Garsdale. The N.W.R. station building has been demolished, but the station house was to remain standing until the early 1970s.

Waiting for the road in the up loop is Stanier 8F 2-8-0 No.8276 of Stourton shed at the head of a lengthy freight working bound for the Leeds area. The 8Fs were regular visitors to Hellifield, and in the 1940s and 1950s a handful were allocated to the shed.

Midland 4F 0-6-0 No.4001 is in typical post-war condition as it passes Hellifield's down outer home signal located by the ex-N.W.R. station. Still in Midland condition, the 4F differs from L.M.S.-built members of the class in having beaded splashers and a Johnson/Deeley tender.

No. 3893, another Midland built 4F, is in charge of a mixed freight in the up loop *c.*1945. The tender is fitted with a rudimentary cab to offer some protection to the foot-plate men when working tender first.

Aspinall 2-4-2T No.10899 is on station pilot duties. These ex-L.Y.R. locomotives were used by Hellifield shed on its local passenger workings along with Fowler and Stanier 3P 2-6-2Ts.

Stanier Black Five 4-6-0 No. 5136 is coming off shed to take up its next working c.1945. The Midland lower quadrant signal gantry controlled the up mainline and loop in the Leeds direction, the signals beyond are those for the Blackburn line.

A long-term Hellifield resident was Johnson/Deeley 3F 0-6-0 No. 3585, seen here entering the shed. Many of the Hellifield crews preferred the 3Fs to the bigger 4Fs, as they were free steamers. The shed starter signal is just behind the tender.

The Stanier 3Ps were more popular with the local foot-plate men than the Fowler or Aspinall 3Ps. No.183 is being prepared on the turntable road judging from the oil cans on the foot-plate.

For many years, the Midland Compounds were the Midland Railway's premier express locomotives. By the time this picture was taken early in 1946, they had been relegated to working secondary expresses such as this Leeds to Morecambe train which is approaching the old N.W.R. station.

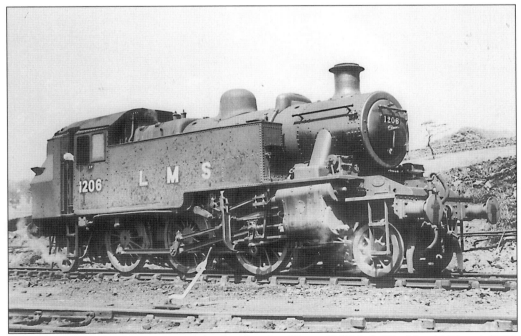

When introduced in 1946, two of the first batch of Ivatt 2MT 2-6-2Ts, Nos 1205 and 1206, were sent to Hellifield. Here, a work-stained No. 1206 is being prepared for its next duty.

For many years, the Stanier 5XP Jubilee 4-6-0s were used on most of the heavy expresses over the Settle & Carlisle. No.5573, *Newfoundland,* is on an up express climbing out of Hellifield towards Bell Busk in 1946. The fireman leaning from the cab is Donald Palmer.

2P 4-4-0 No. 509 is climbing the 1 in 214 gradient to Bell Busk with an engineer's train comprising a flat wagon and ex-Midland clerestory brake third, a light load even for a 2P.

An unusual combination of motive power on a Morecambe working in the immediate post war years is shown here. Approaching Hellifield, L.M.S built Compound 4-4-0 No.1022 is piloting an unidentified Stanier 4P 2-6-4T.

A work stained Stanier 8F 2-8-0 plods up hill out of Hellifield with an up freight. The fireman has built up his fire for the climb ahead. The 8F is carrying a small buffer beam snow plough in deference to the high Pennine weather.

After their introduction in 1935, Stanier 4P 2-6-4Ts began to work into Hellifield, especially from Manchester and Blackburn. No.2490 is on the shed head shunt about to enter the shed c.1946/7.

Photographed by Henry Casserley on 12 June 1947, Stanier 8F 2-8-0 No. 8153 is raising steam outside the ex-Midland shed. Despite the onset of nationalization in a matter of six months, scenes like this were slow to change at Hellifield.

Four

Transition from the L.M.S. TO B.R. 1948-1954

In March 1946 the L.M.S. published a comprehensive modernization plan for Hellifield's engine shed. A repair shop, mechanical coaler and ash plant were to be provided. However, nationalization brought economics to bear and only the repair facility was built. During this period there was little significant change at Hellifield, as L.M.S. signs and paint-work were superseded by those of British Railways.

Photographed by Henry Casserley on 2 October 1948, Stanier 5MT 4-6-0s Nos 5222 and 4909 are on Hellifield's coal and ash pit roads respectively. To all intents and purposes the scene is still pure L.M.S., the effects of nationalization are still to be felt.

Henry Casserley next visited Hellifield on 2 October 1948 and took the next eight photographs. Here, 3F 0-6-0 No.43586 is shunting a goods train out of the high level sidings. The engine carries its British Railways number but the tender is still lettered L.M.S..

Hellifield was never allocated any Black Fives, but the Stanier 4-6-0s were regular visitors. No.4909 is being serviced before taking up its return working. 3P 2-6-2T No.183 is on the turntable road, while one of the shed's snowploughs rests against the toilet block.

Fowler 3P 2-6-2T No.21, a long-term Hellifield resident, is shunting empty coaching stock. The Fowler 3Ps were principally used on the shed's Blackburn, Hawes and Ingleton turns.

3F No.M3186, another Hellifield engine, is engaged in trip working between the high and low level yards. Unlike No. 43586, No.M3186 is in hybrid livery with the temporary 'M' pre-fix and British Railways in full on the tender.

By October 1948, the station is looking a little tired. The down platform canopy is being reduced in length, the glass having already been removed. The L.M.S. name-boards have seen better days and await replacement while 3F No. 43586 gets the road onto the mainline.

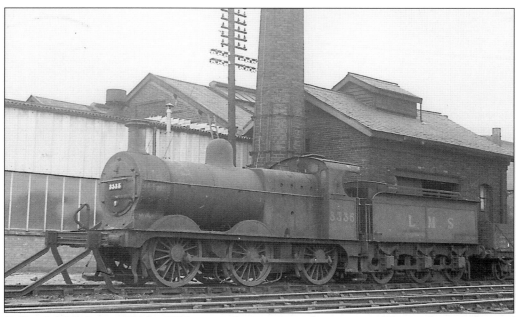

Still in L.M.S. livery, 3F No. 3335 is stored awaiting works attention. The tender is in front of the 1880 sand-house while the 1948 repair shop is the backdrop for the engine.

Hellifield was also allocated some of the small-wheeled Midland 0-6-0s, such as No.3137. The shed's war-time austerity roof is clear in this view, the wooden smoke ducts and chimneys have been replaced by steel tubing and glazing.

The old and the new order of L.M.S. motive power. Midland Compound No.41188 keeps Black Five No. 4909 company. Despite wartime economies, the shed has a well-kept air.

Jim Davenport regularly visited Hellifield with his camera. The next nine photographs were taken by him in June 1949. The first shows ex-L.M.S. Compound No.41056 climbing the 1 in 214 gradient to Bell Busk with a six coach Morecambe to Leeds working.

Dome-less boilered 8F 2-8-0 No.48001 drifts down the bank from Bell Busk towards Hellifield with an unfitted coal train. The driver is looking out for the outer home signal guarding the junction.

Eighteen months after the creation of British Railways, L.M.S. liveried but B.R. numbered, Jubilee No.45659 Drake climbs out of Hellifield with an up express. Numbering apart, the train is wholly L.M.S.

Still in work-stained L.M.S. livery, 8F No.8067 has steam to spare as it slowly accelerates taking an up coke working towards Bell Busk. The motley collection of wooden-bodied private owner wagons is typical of this period.

Hellifield's tender cab fitted 4F 0-6-0 No.44197 coasts towards its home station with a pick-up freight working from Skipton. Such duties were usually entrusted to the shed's 3F or 4F 0-6-0s.

More modern motive power in the form of Stanier Black Five No. 45082, making light work of a long freight train. No.45082 was one of the earliest Black Fives to be built, and still carries a dome-less boiler. The first British Railways livery is also shown to good effect.

Stanier 3P No.183 is on a local Skipton to Garsdale working via Hellifield. Three coach workings such as these were well within the capabilities of these locomotives.

The ubiquitous 4F 0-6-0s were used on all manner of workings. No.44222 is getting to grips with a long up empty mineral working on the climb out of Hellifield. The second wagon is a modern steel 16 ton variant of the traditional wooden-bodied stock that makes up the rest of the train.

Piloted Black Fives were frequently used on the Carlisle expresses when more powerful motive power was unavailable. The Thames-Clyde Express is seen in charge of 2P 4-4-0 No.40488 and 4-6-0 No.M4753 as it coasts towards Hellifield.

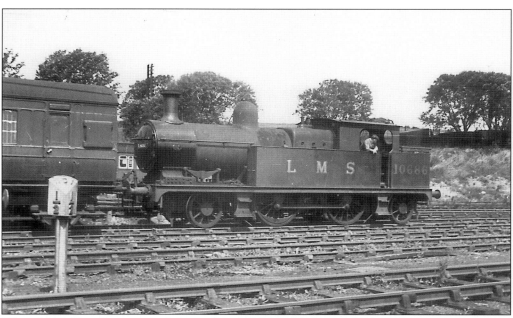

When M N Clay photographed Aspinall 2-4-2T No.10686 on 19 July 1949, it was still sporting full L.M.S. livery despite having received a light overhaul. Waiting in the carriage sidings with empty stock, the grounded Pullman car can be seen between the locomotive and brake third.

On 25 February 1951, 3P 2-4-2T No.50625 has been re-numbered but still carries L.M.S. on its tank sides. The sack covering the chimney shows that the engine is stored pending a decision on its future.

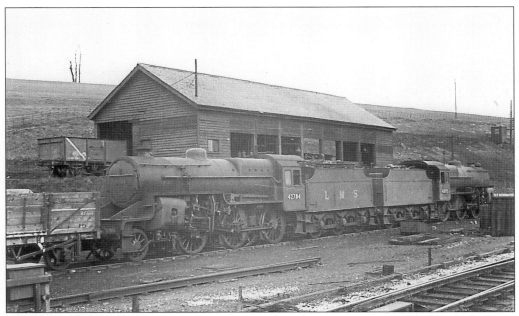

The Hughes/Fowler Crab 2-6-0s were part of the Hellifield scene throughout L.M.S. and B.R. days. Here Nos 42784 and 42875 are awaiting coaling on 25 February 1951 with No.42784 still attached to a tender bearing the legend L.M.S. The wooden coal stage is still in reasonable condition after seventy years exposed to the elements.

A panoramic view of the shed, taken by Henry Casserley on 23 April 1954. South Junction signal box guards the entry to the shed as a 2P 4-4-0 No.40635 raises steam next to the breakdown crane. The water tank hides the offices from view while the wartime white paint has obviously been touched up since 1945.

No. 40632 is next to the white-washed turntable pit, another reminder of blackout precautions along with the lamp standard. The 2Ps were used by the shed for pilot duties and local passenger work. Behind the tender are the break-down riding coaches.

By April 1951 Ivatt 2-6-2T No.41206 is carrying B.R. livery as it leaves Hellifield for Garsdale. The Ivatt 2MTs replaced the various 3P tank engines on these workings. The carriage sidings are to the left.

Ivatt's Class 4 2-6-0s were designed to replace the Midland 3F and 4F 0-6-0s. Double chimney No.43035 is in charge of a down fitted freight. Once fitted with single chimneys and blast-pipes, these 2-6-0s became very popular mixed traffic locomotives.

Approaching Hellifield on the rising gradient from Long Preston, Jubilee No.45718 Dreadnought is in charge of a limited load up express. The engine is coupled to a narrow-bodied 3,500 gallon Fowler tender.

Jim Davenport's portrait of Black Five No.44882 benefits from the late afternoon sun in April 1951. The locomotive is carrying a standard top feed boiler and retains British Railways in full on the tender.

8F 2-8-0 No.48161 drifts down hill towards Long Preston with a loaded train of wooden-bodied coal wagons. The new repair shop is just visible extending from the rear of the shed, while the chimneys of the office block are seen above the ninth and tenth wagons.

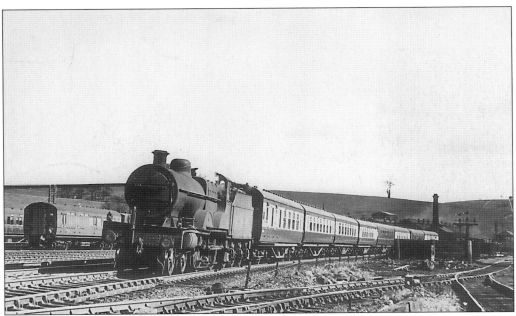

An ex-L.M.S. Compound leaves Hellifield in charge of a Leeds to Morecambe express loaded to seven carriages, five of which are in carmine and cream livery. These residential trains were used by Leeds and Bradford businessmen to commute between their city offices and seaside homes.

Not all the Morecambe trains were made up of modern stock: 4-4-0 No.41067 has a mixed bag of carriages in tow on this Leeds working in April 1951.

The Hughes/Fowler 'Crab' 2-6-0s were often rostered for excursions. No.42767 is returning empty stock from the coast to Leeds.

5MT 4-6-0 No.44963 follows a block behind No.42767 on another empty stock working. The eleven coach train is made up of older L.M.S. stock kept solely for holiday traffic.

Viewed through Henry Casserley's camera on 23 April 1954, platforms 1 and 4 (the up mainline and north bay) are dominated by the inner home repeater signal, necessary because of the up main line curving away to the right, allowing drivers an early sighting of the home starter. The coal stage can be seen to the left.

This view of the empty Blackburn bay illustrates how bleak Hellifield could be on any but the sunniest of days. The up canopy has had the glass removed, but the ironwork stands as a gaunt reminder of better days.

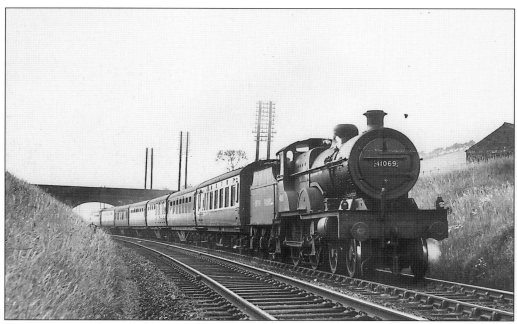

It is now June 1951, and Compound No. 41069 has just passed under the Aireton Road bridge after leaving Hellifield with a Morecambe to Leeds working. The locomotive is still carrying the early B.R. livery.

Ex-L.M.S. Compound No.41118 is passing Hellifield station with a relief Leeds to Morecambe working on 23 May 1953. At holiday times, such as Whitsun, the railways were often hard-pressed to cope with all the traffic they were required to deal with.

It is now July 1953 and Compound No.41056 runs light through Hellifield. Black Five No.44903 is in the Carlisle bay with an all stations passenger working, while an up express is alongside the main down platform.

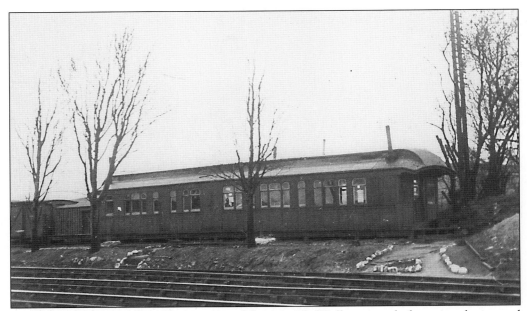

23 April 1954 - Henry Casserley's picture of the grounded Pullman coach shows it to be in good condition still. White-washed stones lined the paths while the saplings in the pictures on page 30 are now mature trees.

R.M. Casserley captured No.41102 at Hellifield on 4 September 1955. The extent to which the platform canopies were eventually cut back is quite apparent.

Stanier 3P 2-6-2T has just returned to its home shed of Hellifield after overhaul and is carrying fully lined mixed traffic livery. Pictured in the Blackburn bay, the locomotive is about to work an all station train to Blackburn.

An unusual visitor to Hellifield is Scottish Region allocated Black Five No.45154 *Lanarkshire Yeomanry*. The locomotive would have worked into Hellifield over the Settle & Carlisle.

Hellifield South Junction signal-box was sited just north of the Carlisle bay. Derek Soames is the signalman watching the photographer.

All but one of the Riddles WD 2-10-0s were Scottish Region locomotives for all their British Railways lives. This view of the exception shows Carlisle Kingmoor's No. 90763 coming off shed at Hellifield. The locomotive regularly worked into Hellifield over the Settle & Carlisle.

Five
B.R. Post-1955

The publication of British Railways' modernization plan in 1955 was a radical attempt to address the problems of the country's railways. However, it was eventually to change the face of the railways in and around Hellifield in particular. Riddles' standard designs began to appear before the onset of dieselization. The engine-shed was closed in June 1963 and demolished in the early 1970s, goods facilities withdrawn and the station reduced in status to that of an unmanned halt in the mid 1960s. Passenger services were withdrawn, starting with those to Blackburn, and an air of neglect and desolation descended on the junction. Eventually the fabric of the station itself began to decay, while only the rosebay willow herb flourished.

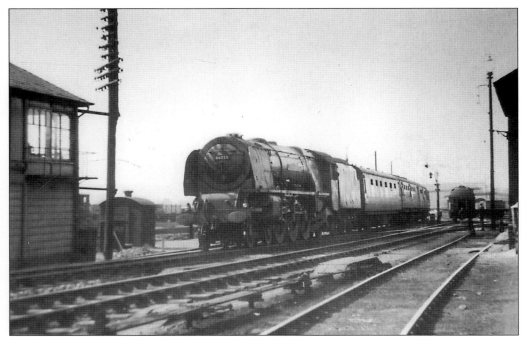

Stanier Duchess pacifics were a rarity at Hellifield. No.46225, *Duchess of Gloucester*, heads a diverted up express past North Junction signal-box. Engineering work on the West Coast mainline had brought diversions via Low Gill and Ingleton to Hellifield.

Stanier 4P 2-6-4T No.42472 is on Hellifield's 60ft turntable, which was installed in 1940 to turn the then-new Stanier 4-6-0 and 2-8-0 designs. Photographed on 23 April 1954 by Henry Casserley, the water tank, workshops and offices are immediately behind the firebox and cab.

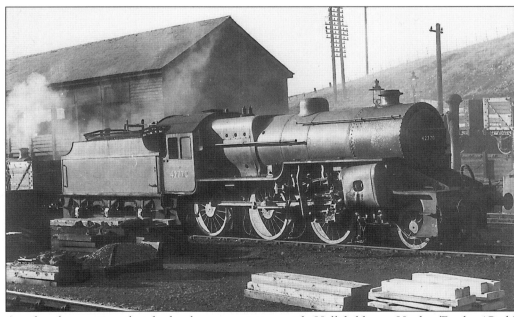

Another locomotive that had a long association with Hellifield was Hughes/Fowler 'Crab' No.42770, seen in the late afternoon of July 1955. These powerful-looking engines were good steamers and versatile, equally at home with both goods and passenger work.

Stabled by the water tank, Stanier 8F No.48616 displays its 20G Hellifield shed-plate. The 8Fs were used on the shed's heaviest freight turns. (B. Webb, Industrial Railway Society)

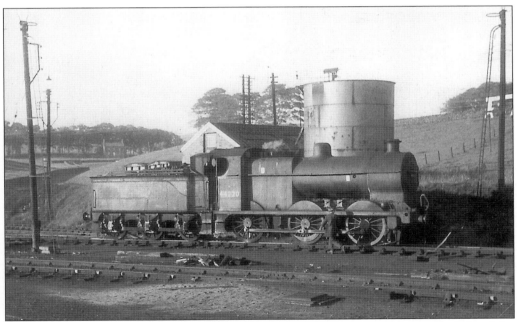

4F 0-6-0 No. 44220 is attached to a Midland tender fitted with a rudimentary cab. Behind the engine is the water softening plant installed by the L.M.S. The electrification warning flashes on the boiler and firebox are clearly evident.

A feature of the last years of steam trains working through Hellifield were the heavy Long Meg anhydrite trains working to and from Widnes. In May 1960, Stanier 8F 2-8-0 No.48321 accelerates an empty hopper train away from Hellifield before attacking the Long Drag after Settle Junction.

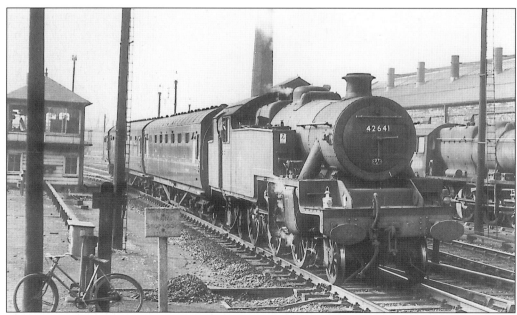

Hellifield's station pilot at work.: Stanier 4P 2-6-4T No.42641 brings the stock of a Liverpool Exchange train out of the carriage sidings in May 1960. 8F No.48274 can be seen stabled outside the shed building.

When re-built, Royal Scot class 4-6-0 No.6105 *Royal Engineer* was put to work over the Settle & Carlisle in the 1940s. It proved itself ideally suited to the route, and the class quickly became favourites with foot-plate men. In April 1961, No.46117 Welsh Guardsman is in charge of the up Thames Clyde Express between Long Preston and Hellifield.

Leeds' Holbeck shed received an allocation of Gresley A3 pacifics in 1960, in order to replace the Royal Scots on the principal Leeds to Carlisle expresses. No.60069 *Sceptre* is on the up Waverley as it leaves Hellifield for Leeds in April 1961.

In the same way that the A3s replaced the Royal Scots, so the Britannia pacifics superseded the A3s. No.70054 *Dornoch Firth* has steam to spare as it takes the up Thames Clyde Express up the 1 in 214 gradient to Bell Busk in April 1961.

7P power was not always available and, in April 1961, Jubilee class 4-6-0 No.45675 *Hardy* is in charge of the down Waverley as it leaves Hellifield behind. With steam to spare, the fireman is hard at work building up the fire for the 1 in 100 climb to Ais Gill.

The inside of Hellifield shed was captured by Henry Casserley on 21 September 1962 with 4F No.44479, 5XP No.45602 *British Honduras* and Hellifield's new steam crane, RS1087/30, in residence.

The inside of the repair shop illustrating the machinery available to Hellifield's fitters. The light and roomy environment makes an interesting comparison with the previous picture.

Stabled on the water tank siding on 8 September 1961 are John Fowler, 0-4-0DM shunter No.ED1 and Hellifield's last 2P 4-4-0 No. 40685. The brick base of the water tower is to the right.

Only weeks before the shed was closed, Riddles *Austerity* 2-8-0 No.90556 raises steam on 4 June 1963.

Caprotti Black Five No.44753 brings a fitted freight down hill into Hellifield. The Caprotti engines were not as well like as the ordinary 5MTs, the drivers believing that they were poor hill climbers.

An up fitted freight threads its way past South Junction signal-box and the engine shed, hauled by 5MT 4-6-0 No.44853. No.44735 is parked outside the shed.

The Riddles 9F 2-10-0s were used extensively in the 1960s on the Long Meg hopper trains. No.92130 is in charge of a loaded train bound for Widnes via the Blackburn line.

Stanier 8Fs were still found on the Long Meg workings after the arrival of 9Fs at Carlisle Kingmoor. No.48472 wheels a loaded train away from Long Preston in June 1961.

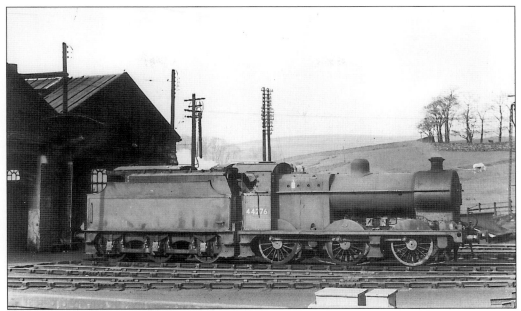

4F No.44276 raises steam outside the shed. One of Hellifield's long term residents, the locomotive, is adapted for snow plough use, the modified tender and securing hole behind the buffer beam being the main modifications.

In the 1960s Riddles 76000 2-6-0s from Lower Darwin shed became frequent visitors to Hellifield. No.76022 awaits the road with an up excursion on 14 September 1961.

The gradual withdrawal of steam locomotives in the 1960s brought many railtours to Hellifield. On 23 May 1964, Clan 4-6-2 No. 72007 *Clan MacKintosh* replenishes its water supply while working the RCTS 'Ribble-Lune' special.

The last Royal Scot in service No. 46115 *Scots Guardsman* calls at Hellifield with the RCTS Royal Scot Commemorative Railtour on 13 February 1965.

Britannia 4-6-2 No.70013 *Oliver Cromwell* stands pilot in Hellifield yard during the mid 1960s. The Settle & Carlisle was used as a diversionary route at weekends, while electrification work took place on the West Coast mainline. Despite the closure of the engine shed, the turntable was still in use.

Another Britannia pacific on pilot duty at Hellifield during diversions. No.70032 Charles Dickens waits in the up loop for its next duty.

By June 1967, steam traction had less than six months left on the Settle & Carlisle. Jubilee No.45675 *Hardy* has steam to spare as it takes a short up parcels working out of Long Preston.

Jubilee class 4-6-0 No.45604 *Ceylon* on a down fitted freight approaching Hellifield in June 1967.

An unusual visitor to the Hellifield line in June 1967 was re-built Merchant Navy class 4-6-2 No.35012 *United States Line* on a RCTS railtour.

Preserved A3 pacific No.4472 *Flying Scotsman* leaves Hellifield with a railtour in May 1967. The disused repair shop is to the left of the picture.

Preserved Highland Railway Jones Goods 4-6-0 No.103 heads light engine through Hellifield on its way south to take part in the filming *of Those Magnificent Men In Their Flying Machines* in May 1964. This locomotive now resides in Glasgow's transport museum.

Six
National Collection Store

After the engine shed closed in June 1963, it was decided to use the shed as a store for locomotives that had been withdrawn but earmarked for preservation as part of the National Collection. The thinking behind this was quite straightforward; the four road building was watertight and could easily be made secure, and it was in a relatively isolated rural location. Unfortunately, this was only ever seen as a temporary measure, and by 1969 the locomotives had moved on to new locations, leaving the way open to demolish the shed buildings.

Midland Railway 2-4-0 No.158A was one of a handful of Midland locomotives stored at Hellifield. The engine left Hellifield in August 1967, and was eventually to move to the Midland Railway Trust at Butterley, Derbyshire.

Great Eastern Railway J17 0-6-0 was restored as L.N.E.R. No.1217E before moving north to Hellifield. After its sojourn in Yorkshire, the locomotive moved to Alan Bloom's Bressingham Steam Museum and, as No. 8217, is on display at the N.R.M., York.

The North Eastern Railway's Bo-Bo electrics, Nos 26500 and 26501, were kept at Hellifield between January 1965 and 11 July 1966. Both are in the North Eastern green livery they were carrying when withdrawn.

The beautiful Johnson 4-2-2 No.118 was another Midland Railway resident. This locomotive, re-numbered as No.673, was to be restored to steam for the 1980 150th anniversary of the Rainhill Trials. It now can be found in the N.R.M., York.

At the other end of the passenger locomotive scale was Gresley A4 No.60010 *Dominion of Canada*, which stayed at Hellifield until Crewe Works was able to overhaul and re-paint it before being presented to the Canadian Government for display in Canada.

Gresley V2 2-6-2 No. 4471 *Green Arrow* was the only one of the stored locomotives to return to Hellifield in steam when it made its first run over the Settle & Carlisle in 1978. Battle of Britain 4-6-2 No. 34051 *Winston Churchill* joined No.4471 in the shed during December 1965.

L.N.W.R. 0-4-0ST No. 1439 was the smallest locomotive kept at Hellifield. Eventually, it was to be cosmetically restored, and was last at the East Lancashire Railway at Bury.

Vying with the N.E.R. Bo-Bo electrics to be the most unusual piece of rolling stock moved to Hellifield was Great Western stream-lined diesel railcar No.4. This art deco-styled vehicle is now at Swindon.

Another locomotive type that was well known at Hellifield was the Hughes/Fowler 'Crab' 2-6-0s. The first member of the class No.42700 is in withdrawn condition. In 1968 the locomotive was moved to the nearby Keighley & Worth Valley Railway, where it was steamed a few times. Now restored to L.M.S. livery, it graces the N.R.M., York.

Viewed from Hellifield's up platform, the engine shed shows no indication of the valuable collection of locomotives stored within its walls.

The eastern end of the station is already taking on an air of neglect. The coal stage has been demolished, but the water softening plant still stands on the embankment.

Seven

Decay and Neglect
1970-1990

After the demolition of the South Junction signal-box and the engine shed in the early 1970s, the station slipped quietly into a long period of decaying hibernation. The windows of the station building were boarded up, and the only passenger trains to disturb the roosting pigeons and starlings were first generation diesel multiple units making their way to and from Carlisle and Morecambe. Freight trains still rumbled through, and so the up and down loops were kept in commission. The Blackburn line remained in use because of its value as a diversionary route. By the 1980s it was obvious to all that British Rail was aiming to close the Settle & Carlisle by stealth and demolish the station buildings at Hellifield, as they were rapidly becoming unsafe due to a complete lack of any kind of maintenance. The creation of the Friends of the Settle and Carlisle Line was to change all this, and the closure of the S & C was defeated. Hellifield's station was declared a Grade II listed building, thus preventing its demolition and paving the way for its eventual restoration. It was a close-run race and one that reflects great credit on the FoSCL and very little on B.R.

The subway entrance to Hellifield station on 23 July 1985. Apart from the signs and posters, this view is little changed from the 1880s.

The isolated location of Hellifield station is only too apparent from this November 1985 view. The landscape surrounding the station has hardly changed in comparison with the picture on page 25.

Looking towards South Junction signal-box in the early 1970s. The rosebay willows herb is rampant in, what was, the Blackburn bay, but the platform lights still retain their opaque glass and enamel totems.

The enamel Platform 3 sign points to the long abandoned Blackburn bay where the platform surface has visibly decayed. The rationalized signalling compares unfavourably with the photograph on page 41.

By 1988 the view from the site of the South Junction signal-box was that of a station which had fallen upon hard times. An air of dereliction pervades the scene.

Pictured from a passing diesel multiple unit, the engine shed is seen just before the demolition men moved in.

Knee-high weeds hide the turntable from view, but the water tower, tank and offices on the northern side of the shed are can be seen awaiting their fate.

The MR monogram was an integral part of the ironwork supporting the glass canopies and remains a lasting reminder of that company.

Seen through the ironwork, Gresley A4 pacific No.4496 *Sir Nigel Gresley* waits in the up loop during the filming of a British Railways television commercial on 1 November 1984.

The Midland's Wyvern heraldic device was also cast into the canopy ironwork, along with the MR initials.

South Junction signal-box is a typical Midland structure which has survived better than most of Hellifield's railway buildings.

28 March 1986: the station buildings show how much damage the Pennine weather has done to the structure. Despite the boarded-up windows, the roof has lost many tiles, the canopy glass is structurally dangerous and the stonework is damp and covered in green mould.

From under the canopy the boarded-up windows of the booking office are opposite the subway entrance. The ticket collector's wooden office is on the left, and makes an interesting comparison with the picture on page 26.

The interior of the booking office in 1986 shows the entrance vestibules and glazed partition walls. The colour scheme is light green and cream.

Located above the refreshment rooms was the flat occupied by the staff. The food lift is between the two doors. The right hand door leads to the bedrooms.

The booking office was latterly used as a mess room for foot-plate crews and permanent way men, but by 1986 had long been boarded-up. The peeling paint is a testimony to water seeping into the fabric of the building.

At one time, the refreshment room was the pride and joy of the station. Disused for over twenty years, it is hard to visualize the roaring fire and boiling tea urn.

The stairs leading from the refreshment room to the upper storey. The ornate doorframe shows the attention to detail in the design of the buildings.

By August 1986 the state of the canopy was giving cause for concern. A survey deemed it unsafe and the areas under the canopies were cordoned off.

In March 1994 work to restore the buildings was in progress. The up side of the station is hidden by scaffolding as contractors attempt to put right years of neglect.

The canopy has been reduced to its structural elements. The building has been boarded up, as the station was still open to passengers on the Leeds, Morecambe and Carlisle lines.

Reduced to a shell, the building was thoroughly renovated and the roof was completely replaced during restoration.

The down platform, seen during the restoration work in March 1994. The wooden huts were not to survive the re-building.

Eight
Diesel Power

Although the lines through Hellifield saw regular steam until the end of 1967, and British Railways' last steam workings didn't pass through until 11 August 1968, diesel traction had been becoming more and more common since the 1950s. The prototype Deltic was tested over the Settle & Carlisle in 195*, but it was the Peak and Class 40 1Co-Co1 diesels that came to dominate the passenger workings through Hellifield. In the three decades since the end of steam working on British Railways, a great variety of diesel power has been seen ranging from the humble diesel multiple units to the Type 5 General Motors Class 66 Co-Cos.

An unidentified Class 40 1Co-Co1 brings an up express into the up platform in the mid-1960s. South Junction signal-box is still standing, and the engine shed houses some of the National Collection.

During the summer months, a Dales rail service was run from Manchester to stations on the Settle & Carlisle. On 26 March 1988, a diesel multiple unit from Macclesfield heads for the hill.

28 March 1988: the second generation of diesel multiple units is represented by Pacer unit No. 144022 on a Morecambe working. The Pacer carries the red and cream livery of the West Yorkshire Transport Executive.

The 10.13 Hellifield to Leeds, the 08.50 ex-Morecambe, begins the climb to Bell Busk on a snowy 4 March 1987. These diesel units were used on these services for the best part of thirty years.

In 1986 unit M54247/M53964 was re-painted with a reconstruction of its first green livery. Coupled to blue/grey liveried unit, the heritage unit forms an all station working to Carlisle.

Class 40 No.40106/D200 became a celebrity locomotive in the mid 1980s, as it was never painted B.R. blue and remained in traffic long after the rest of the class were withdrawn. It was a regular performer on the Leeds to Carlisle trains and is pictured here on an up working.

Class 25 No.25278 is on an engineer's working in the down cripple loop, while Class 37 No.37009 sits in the down loop with a failed diesel multiple unit on 26 August 1986.

A busy interlude on 25 February 1987 sees the 08.50 Morecambe to Leeds departing, as Class 31 31200 waits to run round into the up sidings. In the old high level yard are Pacers 144001 and 142074 on crew training duty.

When D200 was eventually withdrawn, Class 47s took over the Leeds to Carlisle trains. On a wintry 23 March 1989, 47406 leaves Hellifield with the 06.34 Carlisle to Leeds.

Stratford's immaculate 47585 *County of Cambridgeshire* is at the head of the Royal Train on 4 March 1987. The empty train has come from Saltaire, where HRH The Princess of Wales was making an official visit.

A more mundane, but equally important, working finds Class 20 20903 at the head of the Chapman's weed-killing train on 26 July 1989 in the down loop.

Class 25 25278 on an engineer's train waits while green liveried diesel multiple unit M54247/M53964 leaves with a Carlisle working on 24 August 1986.

Equally important to maintaining the track is Matisa tamper 73255, waiting in the down loop at Hellifield on 2 September 1987.

26 August 1986 finds West Country pacific No.34092 *City of Wells* passing through Hellifield at the head of The Pennine Limited. Class 25 25278 has now run round its train in the down cripple loop.

Charter train operators have brought InterCity 125s to Hellifield. 27 June 1987 finds units 43051 and 43072 stabled in Hellifield's down loop.

10 December 1988 finds Merchant Navy 4-6-2 No. 35028 *Clan Line* in the down loop, as Class 47 47406 arrives with the 10.45 ex-Leeds to Carlisle.

IC125 No.253030 on 1 November 1984, during the filming of a television commercial. The HST was labelled 'Our Trains Now Travel A Distance Equivalent Of Going Round The World Twenty-Two Times A Day'.

When engineering work closed the West Coast Mainline, the Hellifield to Blackburn line was used as a diversionary route. On the up platform, a temporary refreshment stall has been set up on 21 February 1987.

Class 47 47431 heads the diverted 14.25 Glasgow Central to Euston working past the site of the ex-L.Y.R engine shed on 4 March 1989.

On the same day, 47537 *Sir Gwynedd/County of Dwynedd* crosses Town End bridge with the diverted 07.07 Plymouth to Glasgow Central and Edinburgh.

Not only passenger trains but also freight workings were diverted through Hellifield. On 3 March 1989 Class 20s 20058 and 20087 are in charge of a train of steel as it passes the site of the one time low-level yards.

Class 31 31200 awaits the road with a diverted train of rails on 25 February 1987. The signal is off for the Leeds mainline.

Almost a year later, Class 31s 31276 and 31312 have the road for the Blackburn line on 30 April 1988 with another diverted train of steel coils.

Even though diversions were running a charter train, the Settle & Carlisle Pioneer passes through Hellifield, hauled by 47456 *Aviemore Centre* on 16 May 1987.

On a sunny 2 April 1988, Class 47 47440 brings the afternoon Carlisle to Leeds train into Hellifield. The disused Carlisle bay is in the foreground.

Class 47 47653 brings a Leeds to Carlisle working into Hellifield. Class 31 31200 is stabled in the down cripple siding.

The diverted Glasgow to Red Bank parcel working of 30 April 1988 comes into Hellifield behind Class 47 47079. The empty space between the up and down lines was once occupied by South Junction signal-box and the track work of the Carlisle bay.

Viewed from the ex-L.Y.R. low level yard, Class 47 47648 takes the diverted 13.27 Glasgow to Poole south on 21 February 1987.

A diverted moto-rail working heads north behind Class 47 47482. The canopy is cordoned off because of the dangerous state of the glazing.

Third generation diesel unit, Super Sprinter 156480, departs from Hellifield for Carlisle in March 1995. The site of the ex-Midland shed is only marked by the two buffer stops in the background.

Class 60 60059 arrives with a train of empty Tilcon hoppers bound for the quarry at Swindon on the Grassington branch. The Class 60 will run round its train at Hellifield because of engineering work being carried out at Skipton on 24 September 1994.

Nine

Preserved Steam
1978 onwards

It seemed that after No.70013 Oliver Cromwell *passed through Hellifield on 11 August 1968 with British Railways' last steam-hauled passenger train, the final chapter had been written about the steam locomotive in Great Britain. However, in March 1978, V2 2-6-2* Green Arrow *returned to Hellifield and the Settle & Carlisle where it worked* The Norfolkman *in typical Pennine weather. Since then, a wide variety of preserved steam locomotives have been seen at Hellifield. Who would have thought that representatives of the Great Western, Southern, L.M.S, L.N.E.R. and British Railways would have all worked revenue-earning trains through this one time bastion of the Midland Railway?*

L.N.E.R. liveried Peppercorn K1 2-6-0 No. 2005 double heads L.M.S. liveried Stanier Black Five No. 5305 past the site of the N.W.R. station on 26 July 1986 with The North Eastern railtour.

One of the smallest mainline engines to work into Hellifield was Ivatt 2MT 2-6-0 No. 46441 on 24 September 1994. The maroon liveried engine is running round the train it has just brought in from Carnforth, before heading north over Ais Gill.

One of the more impressive performers over the Settle & Carlisle has been Peppercorn A2 class 4-6-2 No.60535 *Blue Peter*. On 11 June 1994, the pacific is passing through Platform 1 with an up working.

Perhaps one of the more surprising classes to appear at Hellifield was S15 4-6-0 No.828 on 7 May 1994. The Southern Railway 4-6-0 is drifting into the station with twelve coaches on the drawbar.

Considerable interest was aroused by the appearance of a Great Western King class 4-6-0 over the Settle & Carlisle. On 7 March 1995 No.6024 King Edward II is stopped for a blow up, over enthusiastic firing having blacked out the fire. To date, the King has been a disappointing performer out of Hellifield.

West Country pacific No. 34092 *City of Wells* awaits the arrival of its train on 1 October 1988. The un-re-built 4-6-2 was a spectacular performer over the Settle & Carlisle for the duration of its mainline ticket.

Merchant Navy class 4-6-2 No.35028 *Clan Line* has brought its Cumbrian Mountain Express onto the Blackburn line on 8 April 1989. This movement was necessary in order to clear the mainline platforms for a service train.

The signalman from Hellifield North Junction box warns the driver of Riddles 7MT 4-6-2 No. 70000 Britannia that Daisyfield junction signal-box is shut as the pacific takes the Blackburn line on 7 September 1991.

Running past the site of the ex-L.Y.R. shed and Midland high level sidings is Gresley A4 4-6-2 No.60009 *Union of South Africa* on 7 December 1994. All three preserved A4s put to work through Hellifield, Nos4468, 4498 and 60009 have put up some very impressive performance over the Settle & Carlisle.

The Cumbrian Mountain Express brought many large express locomotives to Hellifield. On 22 June 1991 Stanier Princess Royal 4-6-2 No. 6201 *Princess Elizabeth* climbs towards the site of the ex-L.Y.R. signal-box from Blackburn.

Princess Royal class 4-6-2 No.46203 *Princess Margaret Rose* takes the Blackburn line with a Carlisle to Blackburn special on 4 March 1995. In British Railways' days, the ex-L.M.S. pacifics were only seen at Hellifield when the West Coast mainline was closed for repairs.

Jubilee Class 4-6-0 No.45596 *Bahamas* is passing the site of the ex-L.Y.R. sidings and engine shed, as it hauls its train onto the Blackburn line on 17 August 1989.

Stanier 8F No.48151 is waiting the arrival of its train, 26 November 1988. Coupled to No. 48151 is an Ethel – an ex-class 25 diesel converted to provide carriage heating – in Hellifield's down loop

The world's fastest steam locomotive Gresley A4 4-6-2 No.4468 *Mallard* coasts down the 1 in 214 gradient from Bell Busk on 16 July 1988. *Mallard* was returned to steam to commemorate the 50th anniversary of her 126mph sprint down Stoke Bank.

Gresley A3 4-6-2 No.4772 *Flying Scotsman* drifts into Hellifield past the sites of the Midland engine shed and South Junction signal-box on 12 September 1992, with the Tees-Eden Express. The twelve coach train is typical of the loads worked over the Ais Gill by preserved steam engines.

The locomotive that re-opened the Settle & Carlisle to steam traction in 1978, V2 2-6-2 No.4771 *Green Arrow*. Awaiting the arrival of its train on 4 February 1989, the National Collection engine looks immaculate in lined apple green livery.

The Gresley K4 2-6-0s never worked through Hellifield in either L.N.E.R or B.R. days. No.3442 *The Great Marquess* can be seen working over the Settle & Carlisle on 5 August 1989, and pulling onto the Blackburn line to clear the ex-Midland mainline for a service train. The locomotive carries a wreath and black ribbons in memory of its one time owner, Viscount Lindsay.

One of the most consistent and competent performers over the Settle & Carlisle has been Gresley A4 4-6-2 No.4498 *Sir Nigel Gresley*. On 8 May 1993, the pacific is taking the Blackburn line. The erstwhile Blackburn bay is to the left.

Re-built 4-6-2 No.34027 Taw Valley accelerates down the 1 in 214 gradient towards Long Preston with a Carlisle-bound train on 14 December 1991. It is hard to reconcile the empty track-side with the busy junction of the 1950s, but at least the railway survives.